OUR VOI

SPANISH AND LATIN
OF AMERICAN H

SYLVIA MENDEZ

CIVIL RIGHTS ACTIVIST

PHILIP WOLNY

rosen publishing's
rosen central

New York

Published in 2020 by The Rosen Publishing Group, Inc.
29 East 21st Street, New York, NY 10010

Cataloging-in-Publication Data

Names: Wolny, Philip, author.
Title: Sylvia Mendez: civil rights activist / Philip Wolny.
Description: First edition. | New York : Rosen Central, 2020. | Series: Our
voices: Spanish and Latino figures of American history |
Audience: Grades 5–8. | Includes bibliographical references and index.
Identifiers: ISBN 9781508185321 (library bound) | ISBN 9781508185314
(pbk.)
Subjects: LCSH: Mendez, Sylvia, 1936—Childhood and youth—Juvenile
literature. | School integration—United States—Juvenile literature. | Puerto
Rican women—California—Biography—Juvenile literature. | Hispanic
Americans—Education—Juvenile literature. | Hispanic Americans—Civil
rights—Juvenile literature. | Civil rights movements—United States—
History—20th century—Juvenile literature.
Classification: LCC LC214.2 W65 2019 | DDC 379.2'63 [B]—dc23

Manufactured in the United States of America

On the cover: School desegregation activist Sylvia Mendez is shown here
at the White House in 2011, about to receive an award from President
Barack Obama.

CONTENTS

INTRODUCTION

In February 2011, the East Room of the White House in Washington, D.C., was abuzz for the annual Presidential Medal of Freedom ceremony. The Presidential Medal of Freedom is the highest honor that the US government can give to civilians for doing something important or noteworthy. That year, President Barack Obama bestowed the medal on a group of people that included cellist Yo-Yo Ma, writer Maya Angelou, and many others. Among them was Sylvia Mendez.

Few were happier during the ceremony than Mendez. Sylvia Mendez was a nurse, hospital administrator, and an activist. While her family's contributions to making the United States a fairer and more equal society were great, there were decades of her life when her and her parents were underrecognized for their important activism.

In the 1940s, in California's Orange County, the Mendez family was at the forefront of one of the earliest campaigns to end school segregation in the United States. Describing the scene when President Obama put the medal around her neck to Fermin Leal in a February 15, 2011, article, a teary-eyed Mendez said, "I never could have imagined as a child battling segregation that I would end up one day meeting the president and receiving such a tremendous honor."

Luckily, it was just one of many opportunities for Mendez. She has been able to publicize the story of her family's struggle, as well as that of the many families who were involved decades ago with an effort to integrate Mexican Americans and other children of color into whites-only schools.

President Barack Obama presents Sylvia Mendez with the 2010 Presidential Medal of Freedom in the East Room of the White House on February 15, 2011.

The federal court case, known as *Mendez v. Westminster*, was resolved with a landmark decision in 1947. For many years, however, many people had simply not heard of it, unlike famous cases such as *Brown v. Board of Education* (decided in 1954, which declared separate school facilities for white and black children to be unconstitutional). But the *Mendez* case was an important test run for *Brown* and many other cases throughout the United States that struck down laws that segregated schools and other public facilities, like bathrooms, and businesses open to the public, such as eateries, hotels, and others.

Sylvia Mendez was only nine years old when she and her parents became part of US history. But even by the time she reached her eighties, Mendez had not yet tired of spreading the word about their case. Nor had she wearied of working to spread tolerance and knowledge about the civil rights struggles of not only Latinos but of all people. The story of her early life at the center of the struggle for equal rights, as well as her later efforts to memorialize it, will remind every reader about how important such stories and voices are in a modern era that desperately needs them.

CHAPTER ONE

EARLY LIFE OF A CIVIL RIGHTS ACTIVIST

In the 1930s, the United States was much different from what it is today. Many people nowadays may immediately think of southern states—like Mississippi, Alabama, and Georgia, for example—when they think of the word "segregation." In fact, segregation existed in most states and for many different groups. Separate facilities, like bathrooms and water fountains, existed for whites and blacks in places like Louisiana, but so did separate schools for Latinos, Filipinos, and other Asians in many parts of Southern California.

During America's Colonial era, California and much of the American Southwest belonged to Spain. After 1821, Mexico itself gained independence from Spain, and aside from its current borders, it also encompassed most of modern-day Texas, New Mexico, Colorado, Utah, and California. Spanish-speaking people thus preceded English speakers in these areas for a long time. After the United States was granted these territories after a war with Mexico, more Americans settled the West. It was only after this that nonwhites essentially became second-class citizens in many of these states.

Since 1850, all Mexican Americans native to California were technically citizens. Many more would immigrate to the United States, too. During the later part of the nineteenth century, however, according to the California Office of Historic Preservation, "Mexican

Americans throughout California lost land, status, and power . . .[and] were also quickly outnumbered by a surge of [mostly white] migrants from the Midwest and East Coast."

THE MENDEZ FAMILY

Born in 1916, Felicitas Gomez was a native of Juncos, Puerto Rico, and thus a US citizen. Her family had moved to Arizona,

A farmworker picks tomatoes in California's Santa Clara Valley in November 1938. Migrant work in the fields was a common job for many US Latinos, both immigrant and native born.

where they faced discrimination for their Latino background. In 1928, twelve-year-old Felicitas and her family moved again, this time to Southern California, where they weren't treated much better. They also experienced prejudice there. Like many newcomers, her family worked the fields harvesting crops.

Eventually, Gomez married Gonzalo Mendez, who had lived much of his life in Westminster, a city in Orange County, south of Los Angeles. Born in Mexico, he was a naturalized US citizen. Despite this, he, like other Latinos, experienced discrimination when it came to employment, government representation, interactions with police, and many other areas of public life.

In 1936, the newlyweds welcomed their daughter Sylvia into the family. The family also opened their own café in Santa Ana, called La Prieta, which became financially successful. Gonzalo Mendez's long-held dream, however, had been to own his own farm. He had grown up in nearby Westminster, where he had loved going to school as a boy. But his schooling had taken a backseat when the family's financial needs meant that he had to start working in the fields himself. He was only in the fifth grade when he left school for good. He told his family years later that he vowed he would one day be a farm owner and not just a fieldworker.

BACK TO THE LAND

The United States had stayed out of World War II until Japan bombed Pearl Harbor, Hawaii, on December 7, 1941. The wartime distrust of the Japanese by Americans was great. President Franklin Delano Roosevelt signed an executive order in February 1942 that mandated the expulsion of all Japanese Americans living on the West Coast from their homes and into temporary internment camps.

Japanese Americans bound for internment camps pack their belongings in San Francisco, California, in 1942, overseen by US military personnel. The Munemitsus were sent to a camp in Arizona in the 1940s.

This shameful episode in American history played a part in the story of the Mendez family. The Munemitsus were a Japanese family from Westminster. When they ended up in a prison camp in Poston, Arizona, Gonzalo Mendez leased their thriving asparagus farm of 40 acres (16.18 hectares). Gonzalo was finally running his own farm, though he regretted it was the result of such circumstances.

AN EARLY FRIENDSHIP

The Mendez and Munemitsu families were far more than simple business associates during a tough time. In a May 2017 episode of the *Deeper Learning* podcast from the Orange County Department of Education (OCDE), Sylvia Mendez sat down to reminisce with Aki Munemitsu, one of the family's children.

While Seima Munemitsu and his wife ran the farm, laws passed in 1913 forbid first-generation Japanese immigrants from owning land. So their son Tad (Aki Munemitsu's brother) bought the farm when he was only twelve years old. He was the only family member who was legally allowed to own it because he was a native-born American citizen.

Aki and her twin sister were just six years old in 1941, and Sylvia was five. "We would play so much," Aki said to OCDE. "We had so much fun." Sylvia enjoyed some of the Japanese touches that her friend's family had constructed, including a traditional heated bath, and the usual elements of farm life that children loved, including the animals. Mendez told OCDE, "They had pigs. I remember a black one and a white one, and they had chickens and a horse. They had an owl in this big, beautiful barn . . . we would try to see her at night, or hear her at night."

(continued on the next page)

(continued from the previous page)

An author, Winifred Conkling, was so taken with the story of their decades-long friendship that she wrote a book for middle-school audiences called *Sylvia & Aki*. The story alternates between the experiences of these two girls, who shared a very personal and ultimately historic connection. Teachers around the United States have used the book to show students how people have helped each other to resist racism and prejudice.

OFF TO SCHOOL

School segregation became a fact of life in California in the 1930s and 1940s. In Westminster and other Orange County cities—like Santa Ana, Garden Grove, El Modena, for example—Mexican American and Mexican-born students (and Latinos generally) attended their own schools. Sylvia and her brothers, Gonzalo Mendez Jr. and Geronimo Mendez, attended one of the only two schools in their city, Hoover Elementary. The "whites-only" school in Westminster was 17th Street Elementary.

Sylvia described her school in a C-Span event. Hoover Elementary was next to a dairy farm, and the students had to steer clear of the electrified fence that separated the schoolyard from the farm, or they risked getting shocked. She told Damarys Ocana Perez of *Latina* magazine in 2011

The school had dirt all around it. Next door was a dairy farm where they had cows; one day, one of the students from the Mexican school was playing with a ball, and it rolled over to the fence, which had electricity. She got caught in the fence, she grabbed it and it wouldn't let go of her. She [sic] was just shaking her. The teacher had to tell the dairyman to turn it off.

There was no playground, and the entire school complex was just a two-room wooden building. Mendez told Lesli A. Maxwell of *Education Week*, "We would all be in the same bus, the other children, and they would drop us off in front of the white school, this beautiful manicured lawn, with palm trees, and wonderful playground in the front with swings, and then we had to walk to the Mexican school."

The Mexican school was designed to prepare the children for manual labor and service work. Instead of academics, they were taught skills that included cleaning, sewing, and other needlework. She also told Erin Lashway for the *826 LA* blog that the schools taught them only in the morning: "The students would get out at noon and go work on the farms. Especially in Santa Ana, we had the orange groves, and we had walnuts, so

Shacks lined a street in part of Brawley, California, around 1936, mostly inhabited by Mexican fieldworkers, like the families of many Hoover students. Segregation often meant poor living conditions.

the students would leave to go pick oranges or whatever. And it was all geared for them, so that's the way they wanted to keep us."

Many Hoover students also had parents who worked the fields. Unlike the Mendez family, they lived in *colonias*, Latino areas that were usually completely segregated from white areas. The textbooks that Hoover students used were torn up or shoddy, most of them hand-me-downs from other schools, or were hopelessly outdated.

In addition, while Mexican children were kept out of white schools because they supposedly didn't speak English well enough, neither the fluent English speakers nor Spanish-speaking students at Hoover were allowed to use Spanish at all. Children discovered violating the rule were rapped on the hand with a ruler as punishment.

CHAPTER TWO

CHALLENGING SEGREGATION

The Mendez family was doing well for themselves in 1943. They had up to thirty workers on the farm during peak growing season. The Munemitsu lease had made them among the richest Latinos in the city. Still, the condition of their kids' school bothered them. They decided to try and get them into 17th Street Elementary so that Sylvia and her siblings would have a better learning environment.

THE LAST STRAW

The following year, when Sylvia was eight years old, her aunt Soledad Vidaurri (her father's sister) took Sylvia's brothers and her own daughters Alice and Virginia to enroll them at 17th Street for the 1944 to 1945 school year. Sylvia and her siblings shared some physical traits: dark hair and eyes and a brown complexion. Alice and Virginia had light brown eyes, light hair, and light skin. While Vidaurri's daughters were also of Mexican heritage, their first names were English names, while their last name came from a French ancestor.

A school administrator looked over the children and told Vidaurri that she could enroll her children there. They would fit in, he said, and even told her that if anyone were to ask, they were actually Belgian. Sylvia and the other Mendez children would have to enroll at Hoover Elementary, he said.

Vidaurri became angry at this proposal and took all the children home. If they would not take her brother's kids, then hers would not attend the school either. Sylvia's father was upset. Both he and her mother considered themselves as American as they considered themselves Mexican and Puerto Rican.

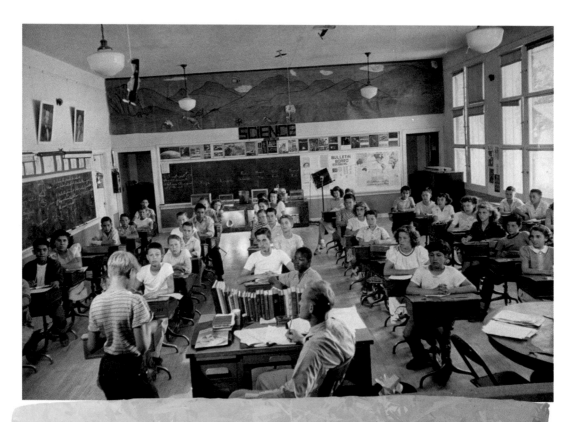

This integrated classroom shows white students learning alongside their black and Latino peers. In 1944, the Mendez family did not find such a welcoming classroom for Sylvia and her siblings.

Still, even as successful farmers and landowners, they were refused service at area restaurants, often told, "We don't allow Mexicans here." If they were allowed, they might sit waiting for a long time, to be served only after white patrons who had been seated after them had finished. They had gotten used to swallowing their pride somewhat and walking away from such situations. But the school's refusal was the last straw for the Mendez family.

In Lancaster, Ohio, around 1938, a restaurant advertises that its owners "cater to white trade only." Nonwhites were not welcome as customers, which would have included successful families like the Mendezes.

PUTTING ON THE PRESSURE

Gonzalo Mendez visited the school to ask the officials if they would change their minds. He had actually attended 17th Street in 1919, years before segregation was officially enacted. But school officials held firm. He went through perhaps every school staff person he could, including the school principal and members of the school's board. The concerned father even took his case all the way to school district officials.

By this time, the family had begun to talk to other members of the community. The Mendezes were not the only Latinos in Orange County who disliked the segregated schools. He had gathered signatures from many of them, along with other supporters. In September 1944, when they turned over a signed petition, the board responded with an interesting solution.

The school superintendent offered to let the Mendez children in, as an exception to the rule. But Gonzalo would not sell out the others for his own benefit. He knew that more minority students would experience the humiliation and unfairness of segregation long after his own children finished school. This family's disappointment and indignity had sparked a movement. He immediately rejected this offer of special treatment. If Sylvia and her brothers were to attend the better schools with the white children, then all the Latino children in their area would, too. And why not all over Orange County and California, too?

TEAMING UP

Sylvia's parents learned about a lawyer making a name for himself as a fighter for Latino rights in California. David Marcus was a Jewish litigator from Los Angeles. He was married to a Mexican woman, at a time when mixed marriages were not as accepted as today. The Mendezes had heard about a case Marcus had argued about segregation of public swimming pools and other public facilities in San Bernardino, a city an hour and a half drive northeast of Westminster. In *Lopez v. Seccombe*, David Marcus had won a decision banning the city from barring Latinos from public pools on days when whites swam.

The Mendez family contacted David Marcus. But they needed other people to help by becoming members of a lawsuit, or plaintiffs. Their stories, and their stake in getting their children a better education, would motivate them and help make the case much better than if it were simply the Mendez family against school and local bureaucrats.

Through word of mouth, and by driving around to meet people in his county and nearby, Gonzalo enlisted the help of several other families. These families included those of Lorenza Ramirez from the city of Orange, Frank Palomino from Garden Grove, and Thomas Estrada and William Guzman, both from Santa Ana. Because of these additional plaintiffs, there would be more evidence to present about the inferiority and unfairness of segregated schools. The different plaintiffs would also help by making it possible to sue several different school districts. Marcus believed that a big victory could help desegregate not

Josefina Ramirez (*right*) was a prominent plaintiff in the Mendez case. Here she receives flowers from her daughter, Phyllis Ramirez Zepeda, at a commemoration of the case's sixtieth anniversary.

only Orange County but influence others as well. This included other possible plaintiffs and elected officials all over California.

Years later, Sylvia Mendez would acknowledge what a big risk anyone fighting segregation took during that era. She said of her parents in Lashway's article in the *826 LA* blog:

THE HUNT FOR WITNESSES

The Mendezes needed to persuade others to fight alongside them. They needed witnesses and support. The Mendezes provided much of the initial money to begin this legal campaign. Felicitas Mendez took on the heavy burden of managing the farm for her husband, as he took a year off to prepare for the case. They combed the regional colonias of Orange County, going door to door and engaging workers in the fields. Would they help them by testifying on their side during the trial?

Many feared the repercussions of testifying. Some (rightfully) feared they could lose their jobs if they made too many waves. Others feared potential anger or even violence from whites in their communities or from law enforcement. Others were undocumented residents and feared being deported. Nevertheless, Mendez, Marcus, and others visited homes, vegetable farms, and citrus groves, making progress, slowly but surely. Gonzalo Mendez even offered to pay for travel and other expenses for witnesses of modest means from other cities during the trial.

They had to stand up against the establishment. My dad—he was being called a communist, and at that time, the forties, to be a communist was something horrible. They were putting people—movie stars, everyone—in prison for being communist. And they were saying he was communist because he was trying to fight against segregation.

HEADED TO COURT

It was March 2, 1945. With Marcus as their attorney, Mendez and coplaintiffs Estrada, Palomino, and Ramirez filed a class-action lawsuit in Los Angeles County Superior Court. A class action can often include many plaintiffs. The lead plaintiffs are considered by the court to represent others, and these others can include hundreds, thousands, or theoretically even millions of people.

The fight for respect and dignity by the Mendez family and their allies would be waged in the Los Angeles County Superior Court, shown here.

The lawsuit's defendants were the collective school districts of El Modena, Santa Ana, Garden Grove, and Westminster. The plaintiffs said that they had been denied "equal protection of the laws" by being denied the chance to enroll their children in the better schools that white students attended. These were the protections guaranteed in the Fourteenth Amendment of the United States Constitution, which had been written to protect the civil rights of freed slaves after the Civil War, but which applied to all peoples, especially marginalized ones.

FIGHTING FOR SOMETHING

For the elder Mendezes, and the other plaintiffs, the things at stake were justice and dignity. For someone young like Sylvia, the reasons behind the courtroom drama unfolding before her were simpler and more naive. In Caitlin Yoshiko Kandil's April 17, 2016, article, Mendez recalls, "We went to court every day, I listened to what they were saying, but really I was dreaming about going back to that beautiful school." She also told NPR's *Morning Edition* program, "I remember being in court every day. They would dress us up really nice. We'd be there sitting really quietly, not really understanding what was going on."

In addition, she knew better than to press her parents too much on the issue. As she reflected decades later, the 1940s were a different time, when children were expected to be quieter and more obedient. Only a little while after the case was settled did Sylvia realize its true importance. It was probably for the best, she thought later, because she did not get the full sense of how stressful the time must have been for her parents. Still, she knew part of the reason her father fought so hard. As she explains in Lashway's *826 LA* blog post, her father "wanted me to be educated. He wanted me to have pride. And to be a polite young lady." Meanwhile, Sylvia actually just enjoyed spending all day with her parents at the trial. Even without having a full understanding of the stakes involved, it was an exciting time for her and her siblings, too.

CHAPTER THREE

VICTORY OVER INJUSTICE

After so much hard work and preparation, the trial finally began in July 1945. Mendez and the other lead plaintiffs were not the only ones counting on the court case. There were about five thousand others who would benefit from the class action suit if they won. David Marcus, as the plaintiffs' attorney, faced off against the lawyer for the school districts, Joel Ogle.

THEIR DAY IN COURT

Many of the arguments of the defense were based on stereotypes of Mexicans and Mexican Americans. The defendants also provided many excuses for why their schools barred or discouraged nonwhite students from attending. Marcus hoped to show the court that their excuses were based on mistaken beliefs, including racist stereotypes. He wanted to demonstrate that children had been mostly segregated, according to Jared Wallace in *Chapman University Historical Review*, "based on their surnames and appearance." Meanwhile, the schools' defense was that many Mexican students had poor English and even were rejected "due to a lack of hygiene."

Sylvia was able to watch and listen every day of the trial because it took place during summer vacation. She was living proof that the schools' claims were simply untrue. Dressed and

For Sylvia and the other children involved, the courthouse where their parents waged their legal battle did seem an important place. Only later, though, did they internalize the case's true importance.

groomed neatly in her best clothing, she spoke perfect English. Another girl, a fourteen-year-old named Carol Torres, also got on the stand and answered the lawyers' questions in English fluently, too.

Some of the children whose testimony was entered into the record brought up an important reason to end segregation. Sylvia and other young people were often made to feel inferior simply because of the fact that they were segregated to begin with. The state of the Hoover school building compared to the modern and neat 17th Street School, as well as the differences in what was taught and what books and other supplies were provided, were signal enough to the children that they were not valued.

This was an idea that Marcus also illustrated by using data from academics who provided more official testimony on how such segregation could hurt the children's futures. Writing in the *Daily Journal,* retired judge Frederick P. Aguirre noted, "Marcus retained as an expert witness Dr. Ralph Deals, head of UCLA's Anthropology department. Deals testified that separating Mexican-American children from 'white' children would stamp the Mexican-American children with a badge of inferiority—and the 'white' children with a badge of superiority."

AN INFLUENTIAL RULING

All sorts of individuals testified on the side of Mendez and the other families. David Marcus somehow discovered an old master's thesis written by James L. Kent, the superintendent of the Garden Grove schools, entitled "Segregation of Mexican Schoolchildren in Southern California." In it, Kent, who was a major witness for the defense, wrote racist falsehoods, such as "the Mexican race is of less sturdy stock than the white race," that they were more prone to communicable diseases, and that they had low scholastic abilities.

The old books at the Hoover School, while still valuable resources, were a powerful symbol of how little these children were respected. Students suffer when their textbooks are outdated.

Amazingly, Kent did little to back down from such sentiments when he was cross-examined by Marcus. It went a long way to convincing the judge and onlookers that school segregation was rooted in racial prejudice rather than simply "community choice."

In the end, Judge Paul McCormick, who presided over the case, sided with Marcus and the Mendezes and the other families. He issued his decision on February 18, 1946. The segregation of students in these Orange County schools was unconstitutional because it violated the Fourteenth Amendment.

When civil and human rights are in the balance, judges and courts wield significant power. Judge Paul McCormick's groundbreaking decision changed the lives of millions of students and their families.

The argument that the schools had discriminated against the children on the basis of national origin won the day. McCormick also agreed that keeping the Latino students out of the better schools in the community would impair their ability to learn English and the values and norms that would allow them to thrive and excel in society.

Within five days of the ruling, the districts appealed the case. In other words, they challenged the ruling, which meant that a higher court would either affirm (agree with it) or reject

WINNING THE APPEAL

The Mendez appeal was sent to the United States Court of Appeals for the Ninth Circuit, based in San Francisco, and that court also eventually agreed with McCormick's ruling, issuing its declaration on April 14, 1947. This would cement *Mendez v. Westminster* as a historic case, make state and national news, and influence legislation in California. The state's governor, Earl Warren, would later become chief justice of the United States Supreme Court and be instrumental in the *Brown v. Board of Education* case of 1954, which declared state segregation laws affecting black students unconstitutional. Thurgood Marshall, a future Supreme Court justice himself, argued the *Brown* case for the National Association for the Advancement of Colored People (NAACP) and used the *Mendez* decision as part of his case.

After the Ninth Circuit issued its final ruling, Warren was pressed to support antisegregation legislation, including signing bills that ended segregation of American Indians and Asians in California.

Earl Warren, seen here in 1948, signed desegregation measures inspired by the *Mendez* case, as well as many later desegregation decisions as the chief justice of the United States Supreme Court.

it. Organized groups of Mexican American parents and community members began to put pressure on the schools involved, including Westminster. Some refused altogether, while others dragged their feet and still others moved cautiously forward with plans to integrate.

Even as the appeals of the school districts made their way through the state courts, an organized effort by many members of the Mexican American community forced the Westminster schools to begin integrating, at least partially. While Sylvia Mendez did not appreciate the full scope of what her parents' case meant during their time in court, it made more sense to her after the decision from Judge McCormick came down.

INTEGRATING INTO THE "WHITE" SCHOOLS

The Munemitsu family was able to return to Westminster in 1946, after the end of World War II. The Mendezes and the Munemitsus worked together on the farm before the Mendezes bought another café and eventually moved back to their old house in Santa Ana.

Sylvia and her siblings, along with all the children in grades one to four at the Hoover school, would move to 17th Street during the 1946 to 1947 school year. Despite her fears about the new school, she found it to be a nice and welcoming place. Both the students and the teachers were friendly. "They treated us really well. It wasn't until we went to Santa Ana, and the case had been appealed in the Ninth Circuit Court in California, and I went into that white school in Santa Ana," she explained in Lashway's *826 LA* blog article, that she experienced some hostility. Because the case was still ongoing, Santa Ana had not yet desegregated, but to avoid controversy and problems later, the white school allowed them to quietly enroll.

For a while after they first started attending school in Santa Ana, she experienced bullying and teasing. It happened the very first day there, in fact, a day she would never forget. She told Lesli Maxwell that a boy approached her and said to her, "'You're a Mexican. What are you Mexicans doing here? Don't you know that Mexicans don't belong in this school. You're not supposed to be in this school.'" These words were so mortifying that Sylvia burst into tears. When she went home, she confessed to her mother that she didn't want to go to this school. She remembers her mother responded, "'Sylvia, weren't you aware of what we were fighting for all this time? . . . We wanted for you to know that you were just as equal as that boy. For you not to feel humiliated, for you not to feel inferior . . . . You're just as good as he is.'"

Sylvia's mother added that she should not be intimidated. She and her brothers took the advice to heart. Even with the prejudice they faced, Sylvia ignored the racist actions of some of her classmates. Instead, she told Perez, "I'd tell the students that we're not born with bigotry in our lives." It wasn't long before one of her brothers was a class president.

CHAPTER FOUR

A TIRELESS ACTIVIST AND ADVOCATE

Felicitas Mendez would continue to wish for a better life for her children as they grew up. In an interview with CNN's Ed Morales, Sylvia Mendez said, "When I graduated from high school, I wanted to be a telephone operator and my mother says, 'we didn't fight for you to become a telephone operator. You have to go to college.'" Being a telephone operator may have been preferable to working in the fields or cleaning houses, the jobs that Hoover Elementary specialized in preparing children for, but her mother wanted her to aim higher.

Mendez took her mother's advice and started at Orange Coast Community College, earning an associate's degree in nursing. She set her sights even higher when she moved on to California State University in Los Angeles. There she earned a bachelor of science degree in nursing, as well as a certificate in public health. From 1957 until 1990, Mendez worked sometimes long hours as a nurse at the Los Angeles University of Southern California Medical Center. Mendez rose from staff nurse to head nurse and then to supervisor. During her last five years at the hospital, she worked as assistant nursing director of the hospital's Pediatric Pavilion. She retired in 1990, partly to help her aging mother, who had become ill in her later years.

The United States Postal Service issued this stamp commemorating the sixtieth anniversary of *Mendez v. Westminster* in September 2007. It featured work by Mexican-born artist Rafael Lopez.

HONORING A HISTORIC FAMILY LEGACY

The court decision that had played such a role in her family history had seemed to disappear into the past. Her father had passed away at the relatively early age of fifty-one. He would not see the full effect of the case on American society. Even most school textbooks and film and television accounts of the civil rights history of the United States left it out.

It was during this time that she spent caring for Felicitas Mendez that mother and daughter spoke often and reminisced. Mendez told Perez:

> It wasn't until my mother was dying that she said, "Nobody knows about this story. It's part of the history of the United States. Everyone knows about *Brown v. Board of Education*, but no one has ever even thanked your father for what he did. And I always thought that a street or something should be named for all he did."

With that, Mendez vowed to her mother that she would spread the word.

As her mother came to the end of her life in 1998, passing away of heart failure in Mendez's home in Fullerton, California, a new life after retirement would begin for her daughter. This was the time that she became a tireless advocate for racial equality and Latino empowerment. A main goal of Sylvia's was to memorialize and publicize the legacy of her parents' actions and the actions of the coplaintiffs of their famous case. She remembered her mother's words to *826 LA* blog: "We didn't do it just for you, but *para todos los ninos* ('for all the children")." These words would inspire the name of a 2003 documentary about the case, *Mendez vs. Westminster: For All the Children*, directed and produced by Sandra Robbie.

SPREADING THE WORD

Mendez did not consider herself a natural public speaker and initially felt awkward and nervous in front of crowds. At first, she felt she had trouble effectively explaining her parents' story. Then a student challenged her when she mentioned "the American Dream," and she could not reply in a satisfying way. It was one of the few times early on that she felt her mind go blank in public. But her natural charisma and enthusiasm soon enabled her to become more comfortable in what was now her life's work. Soon she was visiting schools, churches, community centers, and other public spaces to remind people about her parents' contributions.

Of all public events, Mendez has often said she values engaging with young people the most. Whether speaking before an audience of high school or college students, it gives her

THE MORE THINGS CHANGE . . .

One thing that discouraged Mendez in her travels and speechmaking at first was that many schools she visited were 100 percent Latino—and this was in the twenty-first century! Had her parents' efforts, and those of all the families who fought segregation alongside them, been all in vain? As she related on C-Span, "Imagine my surprise when I started going around speaking, and found out we were more segregated than we were in 1947. Now we have de facto segregation," she explained, referring to a form of segregation that occurs without being mandated officially by law.

It was only after some time, and by speaking with the students at such schools, that Mendez came to terms with

(continued on the next page)

(continued from the previous page)

this fact and was reinspired by the students' optimism and efforts to strive for something better. Many of the students she meets aspire to be doctors, lawyers, activists, and politicians, and to follow other professional career paths. One school she visited was the one that bore her parents' names: Felicitas and Gonzalo Mendez High School, in the heavily Latino Boyle Heights neighborhood of Los Angeles, which opened in 2009. In 2016, to celebrate her eightieth birthday, she was the guest of honor at the school's graduation ceremony. Mendez High School possessed many qualities she respected in a school, including excellent teachers and innovative classes and techniques.

Many of the students, aside from being outstanding scholars, were also extremely proud of their heritage and history, Mendez pointed out. They were knowledgeable about Latinos' legacy and struggles in the United

States and their contributions, which she noted was different from when she was growing up. They were also fluent in English and Spanish, while her own Spanish was rustier than her English.

Sixth-grade students laugh in class at the Gonzalo and Felicitas Mendez Fundamental Intermediate School in Santa Ana, one of several Southern California learning institutions named after the civil rights pioneers.

hope and motivation to continue when they respond well and enthusiastically to her message.

KEEPING THE DREAM ALIVE

Making public appearances is not the only way Mendez has continued to maintain awareness of her parents' efforts and to fight for Latino equality. According to *826 LA*, for example, students from Felicitas and Gonzalo Mendez High School collaborated with 826 LA's writing program to produce an anthology of pieces they wrote themselves, entitled *We Are Alive When We Speak for Justice*. Mendez told Erin Lashway for *826 LA*, "I see it as a great gift for our students to become authors of a book that allows them to talk about their deepest concerns, their families, and what they want in life."

Her efforts—and those of her parents—have gotten more attention in the last two decades than they received during much of the later twentieth century. Sylvia has even met two US presidents as part of her journey. The first was President George W. Bush, whose administration invited Mendez to the White House as part of National Hispanic Heritage Month in 2004.

Even more exciting for Mendez personally was her White House ceremony to receive the Presidential Medal of

Mendez family members are seen here outside the White House following the 2004 Hispanic Heritage Month event (*from left*): Gonzalo Mendez Jr., Sandra Duran, Sylvia Mendez, and Jerome Mendez.

Freedom from President Barack Obama in 2011. At the event, the president told the crowd, "She has made it her mission to spread her message of tolerance and opportunity to children of all backgrounds and all walks of life." She found it fitting that Obama's rise would perhaps not have happened without the efforts of activists like her parents and those who fought for desegregation in *Brown v. Board of Education*.

Mendez explained her dedication to Lashway in the *826 LA* article:

> As a child, seeing how hard my parents worked for my siblings and me, just to be turned away from a school, an education afforded to others, because of the color of our skin, was devastating. Then, to witness the fight and determination that my parents and other families were willing to go through was inspiring. It gave me hope and a sense of pride. I knew that someday I would need to continue their journey.

For Mendez, it was the firm foundation and love that her parents gave her, and their dedication to their cause, that has kept her going. Even when she began her career as an activist and speaker two decades ago, there were naysayers who did not believe that her parents played as important a role as she claimed. Such accusations hurt Mendez, but her mother kept her focused and resilient.

She continues to dedicate her time, even well into her eighties, to spreading the word about how important education is, especially to those who are looked upon as different. This is true for Latinos and members of other minority communities. It is a message she hopes will be taken up not just by the strangers she encounters but by her own family. Mendez has two adopted daughters, who have had their own children, providing her with a big family with four grandchildren of her own.

TIMELINE

January 1, 1936 Sylvia Mendez is born in Santa Ana, California.

1943 The Mendez family leases the Munemitsu farm in Westminster.

1944 The Mendez children are refused enrollment at the 17th Street School.

February 18, 1946 Judge McCormick declares the segregation of Orange County schools unconstitutional.

1946 The schools appeal the decision.
The Munemitsu family returns to Westminster.

1947 The final appeals court decision in *Mendez v. Westminster* comes down, affirming the earlier ruling.
Sylvia and her siblings enroll at the integrated 17th Street School. They are later enrolled at the formerly all-white school in Santa Ana.

1964 Gonzalo Mendez passes away at age fifty-one.

1990 Mendez retires after a thirty-three-year nursing career, partly to care for her ailing mother.

1998 Felicitas Gomez passes away in Sylvia Mendez's Fullerton, California, home.

2000 The Gonzalo and Felicitas Mendez Intermediate Fundamental School opens in Santa Ana, California.

2003 The documentary *Mendez vs. Westminster: For All the Children* debuts on California public television.

2004 As part of Hispanic Heritage Month (September 15 to October 15), the George W. Bush White House invites Sylvia Mendez as one of its guests of honor.

2007 The United States Postal Service (USPS) honors the sixtieth anniversary of the *Mendez* case with a commemorative stamp.

2009 The Felicitas and Gonzalo Mendez High School opens in Boyle Heights, Los Angeles.

2011 Mendez makes her second White House visit, this time to receive the Presidential Medal of Freedom from President Barack Obama for her activism.

2016 The Los Angeles City Council declares Mendez a Latino Heritage Month honoree for her education advocacy and activism.

GLOSSARY

anthology A collection of stories, articles, or other written work, often by a group of different writers.

appeal In a court case, the process by which a party can ask a higher court to change a court decision or ruling.

class action Refers to a legal case in which a greater number of plaintiffs are represented by a single plaintiff or group of them. The members of a class action suit benefit from any rulings that benefit the winners of the suit.

colonia A segregated part of a town or other area where mostly or only Latinos or nonwhites reside.

communicable Refers to illnesses that can be transferred from one person to another.

communist A believer in a system of government in which people, especially workers and farmers, own everything in common. Many activists in the twentieth century, whether communists or not, were called communists in order to persecute them.

de facto Refers to segregation that happens without being officially mandated by law.

hygiene Practices, like bathing or brushing one's teeth, that keep someone clean, presentable, and healthy.

internment Being held as a prisoner, especially for political reasons.

lease To rent or otherwise use a property or business without purchasing it.

manicured Refers to a piece of property, like a garden or lawn, that is neatly maintained.

manual labor Work that is done with one's hands.

naturalized Refers to someone who was born elsewhere but has become an official citizen of his or her new home.

naysayer A person who expresses negative views or believes that something is ridiculous or impossible.

plaintiff The person in a lawsuit or court case who brings the case against another party.

repercussions The results of doing something, usually negative.

resilient Able to handle or withstand difficulties, or recover quickly from them.

tolerance The ability or willingness to accept something different, whether it be different ideas or the presence of people of different backgrounds, religions, or ethnicities.

undocumented A person who resides in a place without official permission to be there legally.

Canadian Hispanic Bar Association (CHBA)

c/o Singer Kwinter
1033 Bay Street, Suite 302
Toronto, ON M5S 3A5
Canada
Website: http://www.c-hba.net
Facebook: @CHBAlaw
Twitter: @CHBA_Law
The nonprofit Canadian Hispanic
    Bar Association organizes
    Latin American and Hispanic
    lawyers and law students
    across Canada to create a
    community-strengthening
    group.

Latino Canadian Cultural Association (LCCA)

61 Elm Grove Avenue, Suite 206
Toronto, ON M6K 2J2
Canada
Email: info@lcca-toronto.com
Website: http://www.lcca
    -toronto.com
The LCCA, a nonprofit,
    dedicates its work to creating
    a supportive network for
    Latin American artists in "the
    greater Canadian community
    through its programming
    of contemporary visual

arts exhibitions and
multidisciplinary cultural
events."

League of United Latin American Citizens (LULAC)

1133 19th Street NW, Suite 1000
Washington, DC 20036
(202) 833-6130
Website: https://lulac.org
Facebook: @lulac.national.dc
Twitter: @LULAC
LULAC was founded in 1929,
    making it the country's "oldest
    and most respected Hispanic
    civil rights organization."
    LULAC strives to improve
    the economic conditions,
    opportunities, and much
    more for the Hispanic
    population of the United
    States.

Mexican American Legal Defense and Educational Fund (MALDEF)

634 South Spring Street, #1100
Los Angeles, CA 90014
(213) 629-2512
Website: http://www.maldef.org
Facebook and Twitter: @MALDEF
The Mexican American Legal

Defense and Educational Fund (MALDEF) is a national nonprofit civil rights organization formed in 1968 to protect the rights of Latinos in the United States.

Mi Familia Vota

1710 E Indian School Road, Suite 100
Phoenix, AZ 85016
(602) 263-2030
Website: http://www .mifamiliavota.org
Facebook and Twitter: @MiFamiliaVota
Instagram: @mifamiliavota
YouTube: Mi Familia Vota
The national Mi Familia Vota organization works to encourage voter engagement in elections at every level of government.

National Association for Chicana and Chicano Studies (NACCS)

PO Box 720052
San Jose, CA 95172
Website: https://www.naccs .org/naccs/default.asp
Facebook and Twitter: @NACCSorg

Since 1972, the National Association for Chicana and Chicano Studies has supported "academic programs, departments, and research centers that focus on issues pertaining to Mexican Americans, Chicana/os, and Latina/os."

UnidosUS

1126 16th Street NW, Suite 600
Washington, DC 20036
(202) 785-1670
Website: https://www.unidosus .org
Facebook: @weareunidosus
Twitter: @WeAreUnidosUS
Founded in 1968 as the National Council of La Raza (NCLR), UnidosUS describes its work best: "Together we will build a stronger America by creating opportunities for Latinos. We envision an America where economic, political, and social advancement is a reality for all Latinos, where all Hispanics thrive, and where our community's contributions are recognized."

FOR FURTHER READING

Arkham, Thomas. *Latino American Civil Rights*. Broomall, PA; Mason Crest, 2013.

Barghoorn, Linda. *Dolores Huerta: Advocate for Women and Workers*. New York, NY: Crabtree Publishing, 2017.

Barrington, Richard. *Sonia Sotomayor: The Supreme Court's First Hispanic Justice*. New York, NY: Britannica Educational Publishing, 2015.

Coy, Cissie, and Gabriela Baeza Ventura. *Dennis Chávez: The First Hispanic US Senator*. Houston, TX: Piñata Books/Arte Público Press, 2017.

Cruz, Barbara. *The Fight for Latino Civil Rights*. New York, NY: Enslow Publishing, 2013.

Hansen, Grace. *Cesar Chavez: Latino American Civil Rights Activist*. Minneapolis, MN: ABDO Kids, 2016.

Honders, Christine. *Mexican American Civil Rights Movement*. New York, NY: PowerKids Press, 2017.

Kingston, Anna. *Respecting the Contributions of Latino Americans*. New York, NY: PowerKids Press, 2013.

Koya, Lena, and Alexandra Hanson-Harding. *Female Activists*. New York, NY: Rosen Publishing, 2017.

Palmer, Bill. *Trailblazing Latino Americans*. Philadelphia, PA: Mason Crest Publishers, 2013

BIBLIOGRAPHY

Aguirre, Frederick P. "California Ruling Helped Pave the Way for *Brown v. Board of Education*." *Daily Journal*, November 28, 2017. https://www.dailyjournal.com/articles/344983-california -ruling-helped-pave-the-way-for-brown-v-board-of-education.

Arellano, Gustavo. "OC's Famous Desegregation Case Finally Gets Its Historical Due, But One Family Feels Left Out." *OC Weekly*, November 5, 2009. http://www.ocweekly.com/news /ocs-famous-desegregation-case-finally-gets-its-historical -due-but-one-family-feels-left-out-6431272.

Blackstock, Joe. "Pivotal San Bernardino Case Fought Discrimination Against Latinos." *Daily Bulletin*, June 29, 2015. https://www.dailybulletin.com/2015/06/29/pivotal-san -bernardino-case-fought-discrimination-against-latinos.

C-Span.org. "Sylvia Mendez on Mendez v. Westminster School District." October 21, 2016. https://www.c-span.org/video /?417233-1/sylvia-mendez-discusses-mendez-v-westminster.

Hanigan, Ian. "The Deeper Learning Podcast: Aki's Story: On Relocation and Resilience." OCDE Newsroom, May 8, 2017. http://newsroom.ocde.us /the-deeper-learning-podcast-akis-story.

Hernandez, Greg. "Daughter: Mendez Died Content That Accomplishments Will Live." *Los Angeles Times*, April 16, 1998. http://articles.latimes.com/1998/apr/16/local/me-39922.

Kandil, Caitlin Yoshiko. "How O.C. Parents Laid the Groundwork for School Desgregation in the U.S." *Los Angeles Times*, April 20, 2016. http://www.latimes.com/local/education/la-me -mendez-segregation-20160420-story.html.

Lashway, Erin. "#826LACelebratesHistory: Yareli Rojas' 'Legacy.'" *826 LA* blog, February 3, 2016. http://826la .org/826lacelebrateshistory-yareli-rojas-legacy.

Lashway, Erin. "We Are Alive When We Speak for Justice." 826LA.org, February 1, 2016. http://826la.org/we-are-alive

-when-we-speak-for-justice-a-foreword-by-sylvia-mendez.

Leal, Fermin. "Desegregation Landmark has O.C. Ties." *Orange County Register*, March 21, 2007. https://www.ocregister .com/2007/03/21/desegregation-landmark-has-oc-ties.

Leal, Fermin. "O.C. Civil Rights Icon Mendez Awarded Medal of Freedom." *Orange County Register*, February 15, 2011. https://www.ocregister.com/2011/02/15 /oc-civil-rights-icon-mendez-awarded-medal-of-freedom.

Maxwell, Lesli A. "Sylvia Mendez and California's School Desegregation Story." *Education Week*, May 16, 2014. http:// blogs.edweek.org/edweek/learning-the-language/2014/05 /sylvia_mendez_and_californias_.html.

Morales, Ed. "The School Desegregation Case You Didn't Know." CNN, February 3, 2012. http://inamerica.blogs .cnn.com/2012/02/03/an-important-latino-civil-rights -victory-born-from-a-mexican-puerto-rican-alliance.

Norwood, Robyn. "70 Years Later, O.C. School Desegregation Case Echoes on Campus." Chapman University blogs, September 26, 2017. https://blogs.chapman.edu /news-and-stories/2017/09/26/70-years-school -desegregation-mendez-westminster

NPR. "When Family History Overlaps With U.S. History." *Morning Edition*, produced by Nadia Reiman. March 26, 2010. https:// www.npr.org/templates/story/story.php?storyId=12517140.

Perez, Damarys Ocana. "Medal of Freedom Recipient Sylvia Mendez Is Ready for Her Closeup." *Latina*, February 8, 2011. http://www.latina.com/lifestyle/-news /medal-freedom-recipient-sylvia-mendez-ready-her-closeup.

Strum, Philippa. *Mendez v. Westminster: School Desegregation and Mexican-American Rights* (Landmark Law Cases and American Society). Lawrence, KS: University Press of Kansas, 2010.

INDEX

ABOUT THE AUTHOR

Philip Wolny is a writer and editor from Queens, New York. His work for young-adult readers includes many works documenting stories of activism, social movements, history, and the arts, including *The Underground Railroad: A Primary Source History of the Journey to Freedom*, *African American Entrepreneurs: Stories of Success*, and *Muslims Around the World Today*, among others.

PHOTO CREDITS

Cover Brooks Kraft/Corbis Historical/Getty Images; pp. 4–5 (background) Kyrssia Campos/Getty Images; p. 5 Alex Wong/Getty Images; pp. 7, 15, 23, 30 (background) Molodec/Shutterstock.com; p. 8 Science & Society Picture Library/Getty Images; pp. 10, 27 PhotoQuest/Archive Photos/Getty Images; p. 13 Photo 12/Universal Images Group/Getty Images; p. 16 Allan Grant/The LIFE Picture Collection/Getty Images; p. 17 Interim Archives/Archive Photos/Getty Images; p. 19 Allen J. Schaben/Los Angeles Times/Getty Images; p. 21 Frazer Harrison/Getty Images; p. 24 Panoramic Images/Getty Images; p. 25 jodiecoston/E+/Getty Images; p. 26 Maren Winter/EyeEm/Getty Images; p. 31 Nature and Science/Alamy Stock Photo; p. 34 Rick Loomis/Los Angeles Times/Getty Images; p. 35 MCT/Tribune News Services/Getty Images.

Design: Michael Moy; Layout: Raúl Rodriguez; Editor and Photo Researcher: Heather Moore Niver